The Book of Megan
And Creative Ramblings
By Cherish Fultz

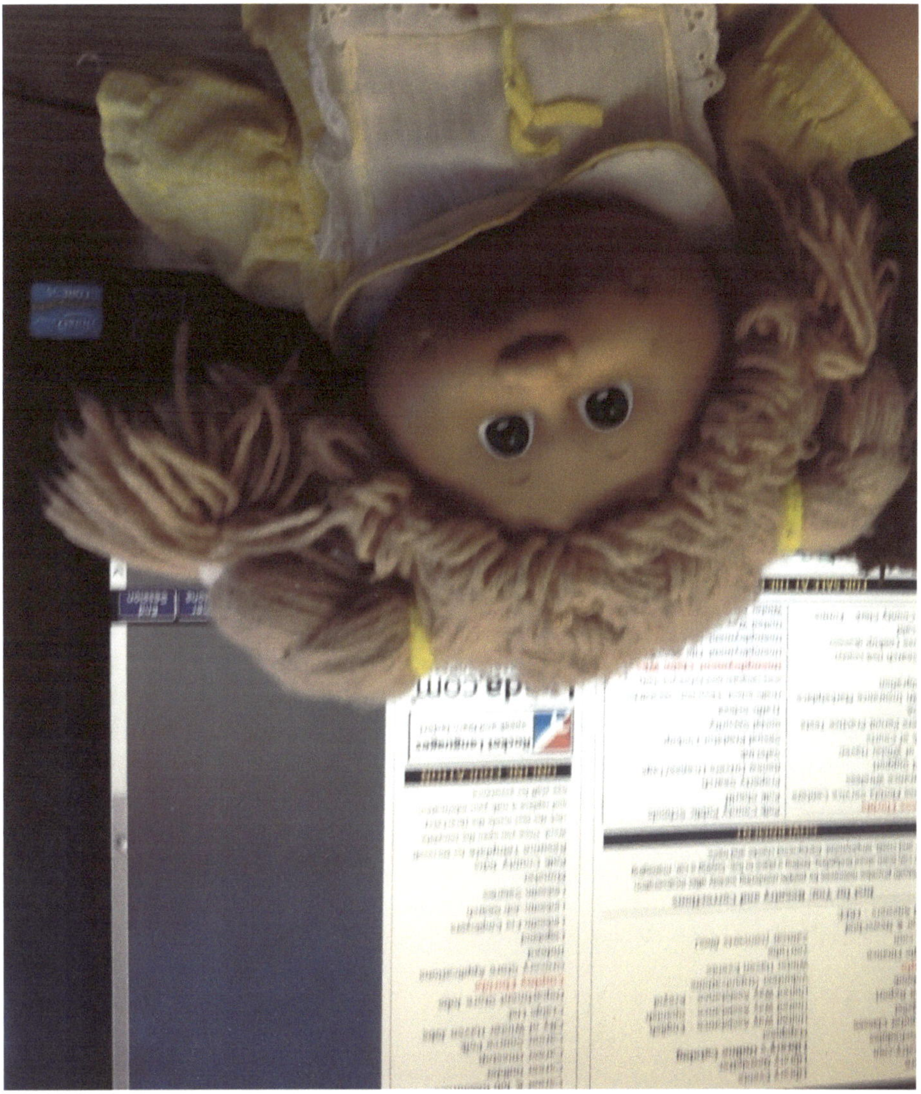

We were having a quiet night at the library, so I was able to persuade mom to relax a bit and Megan to consent to a photo shoot. I could tell that they both wanted to play, so this has become a gallery of Megan, but also a gallery of Mom's creative processes, of sorts. We go to the local library to edit our books. It is the part of the process that we have the most difficult time doing, for it is separate from the joys of creating and completion and consists mainly of painful chopping and changing of words. We love writing, and we love giving our works out to be read, but the editing part is not easy and it takes great discipline on our parts to make it happen. We do the best that we can, and we know that we miss some things, but it all for the love of the books, which are our children.

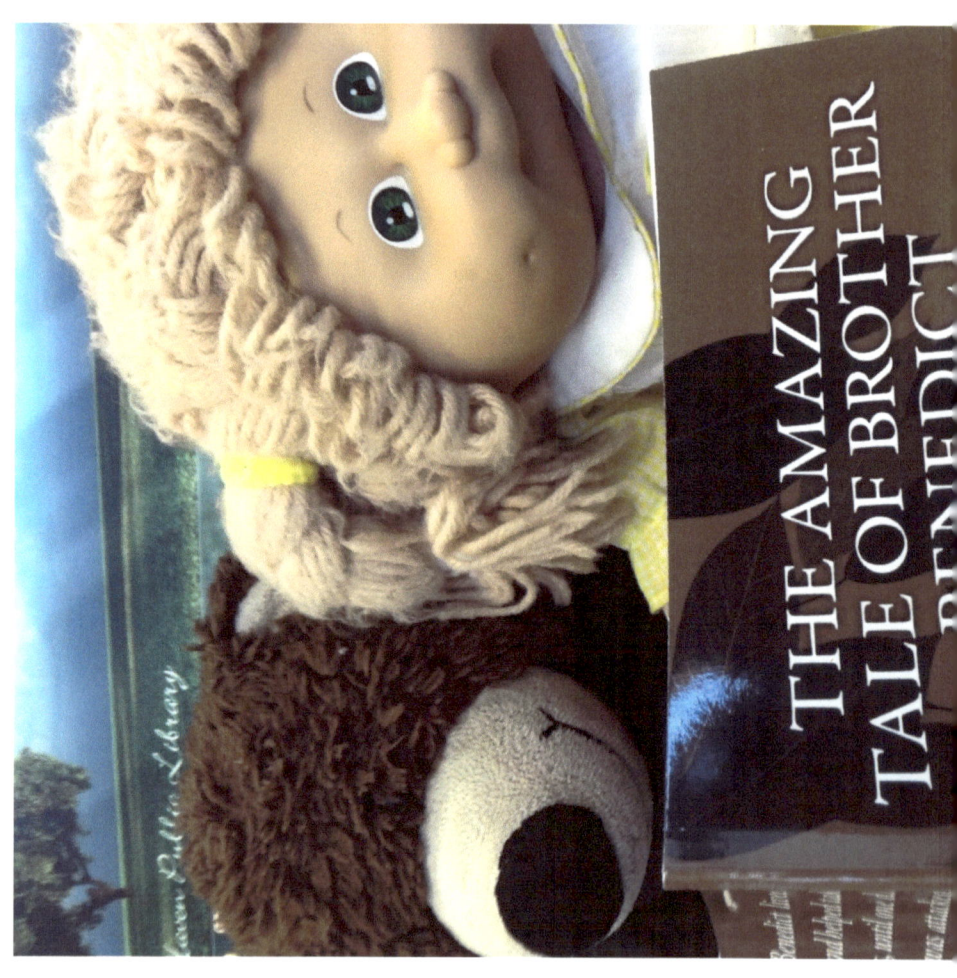

Here we are working on editing a proof copy of The Amazing Tale if Ian Brown, Book Three of the

Amazing Tale Series. Mom dreamt of these books years ago and has been trying to write them ever since. In her dream, each book featured a different character in the werewolf saga and their role in the creation of what becomes a large, beautiful, and hopefully, interesting family saga.

The third and fourth book are proving to smaller than the second, and definitely the first, but we have begun thinking of the fifth book to write during National Novel Writing month in November or NaNoWriMo. Hopefully that will be longer again.

Spoiler alert, Mom has been working on the idea since June and it includes another Plague Doctor who may or may not make friends with our vampire Plague Doctor Phineas Phillips from our vampire novel, Midnight Madness and his apprentice, as immortals of an as yet indeterminate state. This would be Doctor Severus Paine and Cyan, and she is writing a journal for Severus and posting the pages on social media.

She is also writing on another character journal. It is someone who will also be an immortal of some kind in this book. The character is an infantry man fighting during WWII. His name is Jerome Patrick, or J. P. Jones. Jones has a fascination with the mind and observes the effect of the war on those fighting in it, especially any cases he observes of shell shock.

Jones also gets a strange fascination of the middle ages, the black plague and the roles of the plague doctors. He begins to hallucinate, or get haunted by a plague doctor character who gives him advice and actually helps save his life on several occasions. It is Severus, of course, and the reader is left to decide how real this experience is to Jones an in relation to his story.

How these two become a part of the story…..well we can't give too much away, can we?

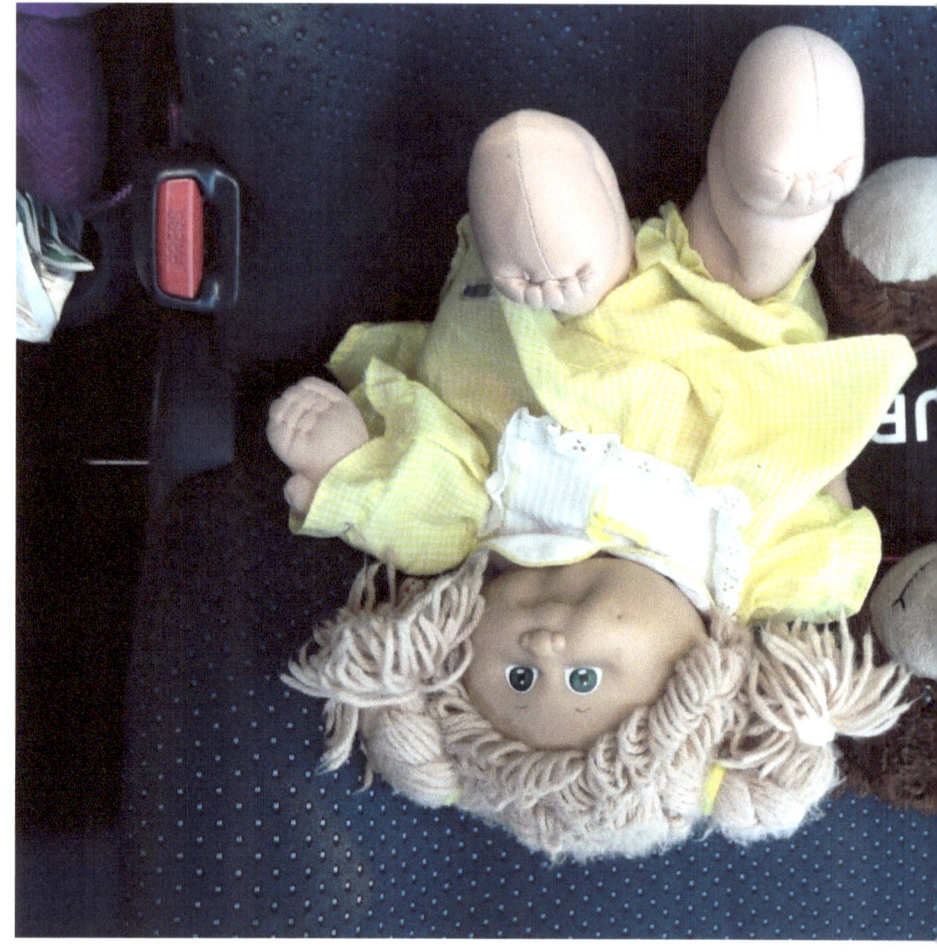

Here is Megan and I in Mom's little room at work. She watches heart rhythms at a local hospital, twelve hours a night. Sometimes, while we are here, we will get an idea of a book or an idea on how to proceed with one of our many projects that we are always working on. At any given time, there are usually several books waiting to be completed, and or edited.

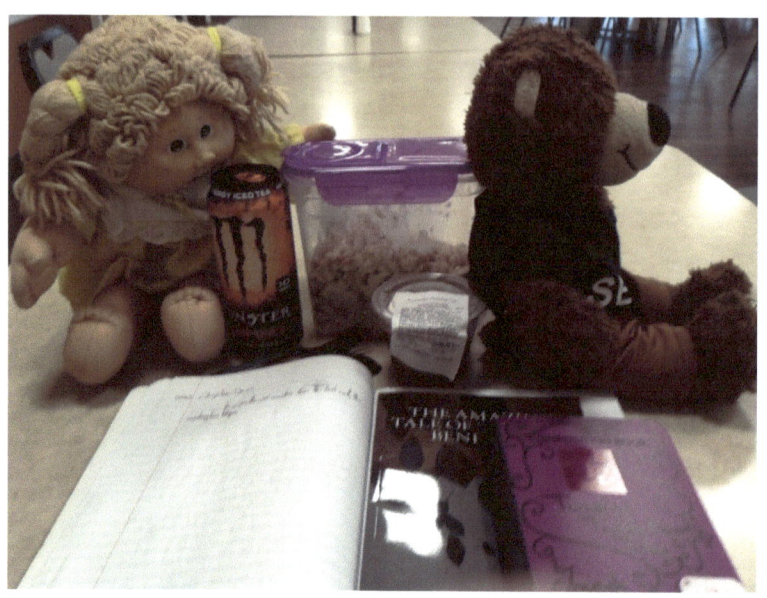

This is us taking a blank space of counter at the hospital while Mom works. We need to edit on Book three of The Amazing Tale Series and finish book four. She made lunch. It looks like a tofu helper, and bought a chocolate pudding and a monster peach tea to go with it.

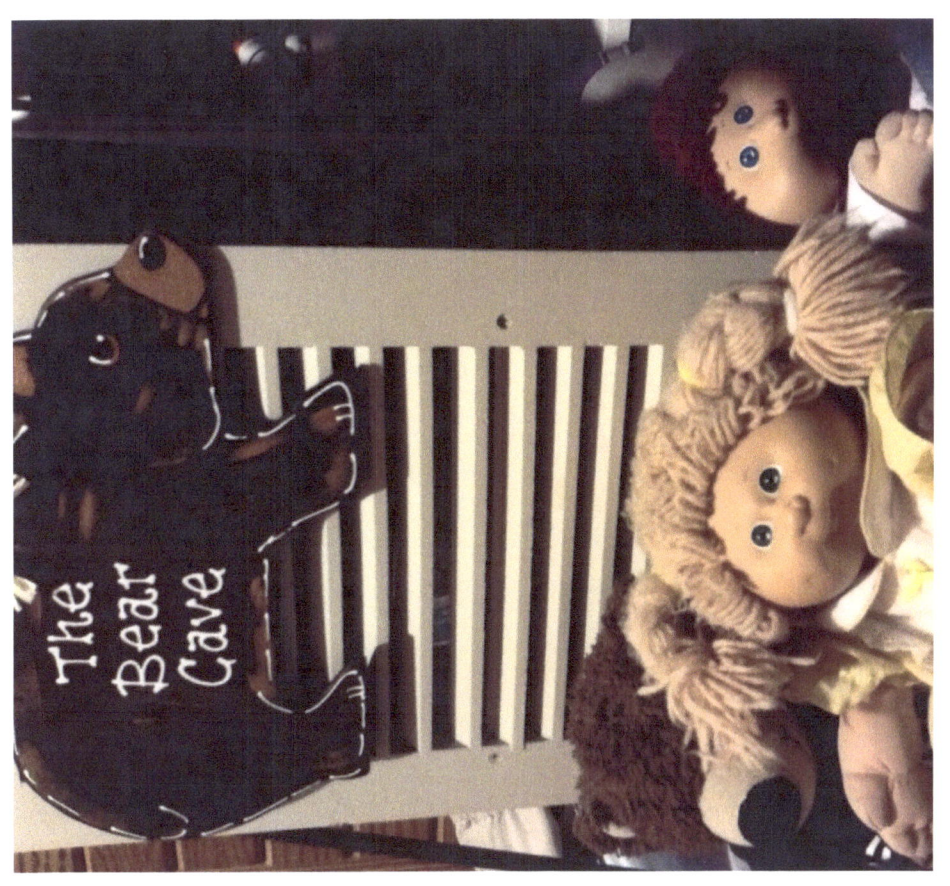

Here we are in a secret space that Mom affectionally calls "The Bear Cave. We get a lot of writing done in here. Also we keep a copy of all our finished works in here and also works in progress which are resting while we are waiting for the right inspiration.

The latter includes our controversial work, "In Her Shoes" which you may or may not read someday. It is a terrible story of child abuse and the cycle in which the abused grows up to be the abuser. Whether or not it gets released, it will hopefully be finished and hidden in this secret location.

Also, there is a book called Ynot2K, about a family who had prepared for the end of the world back in the year 2000, and dropped off the grid.

A generation later, they are still there, unaware that the world has lived on without them. The main character is a trangender teen trying to come to terms with his life in a world where he cannot change his outer form to meet his inner mind, as he is excommunicated from the community, to find the world is not at all what it seems. You may, or may not read this someday, but we hope to at least finish a copy of it to be hidden.

This November, we will be working on The Amazing Tale of Ancient Cyan, which is Book five of the amazing Tale Series. This Book will follow Cyan, the self-named assistant of the Plague Doctor, Doctor Severus Paine, and a friend of the WWII infantry man, J.P. Jones, all of whom have obtained a type of immortality and is trying to broker a peace treaty with the Severson house and the Phillips home of the werewolf Series and of Midnight Madness.

We like to connect our books together in the same world whenever possible, even if one book exists in another word as a book.

In this case, the vampires and werewolves and other immortals all live in the same universe and will be brought together in later books.

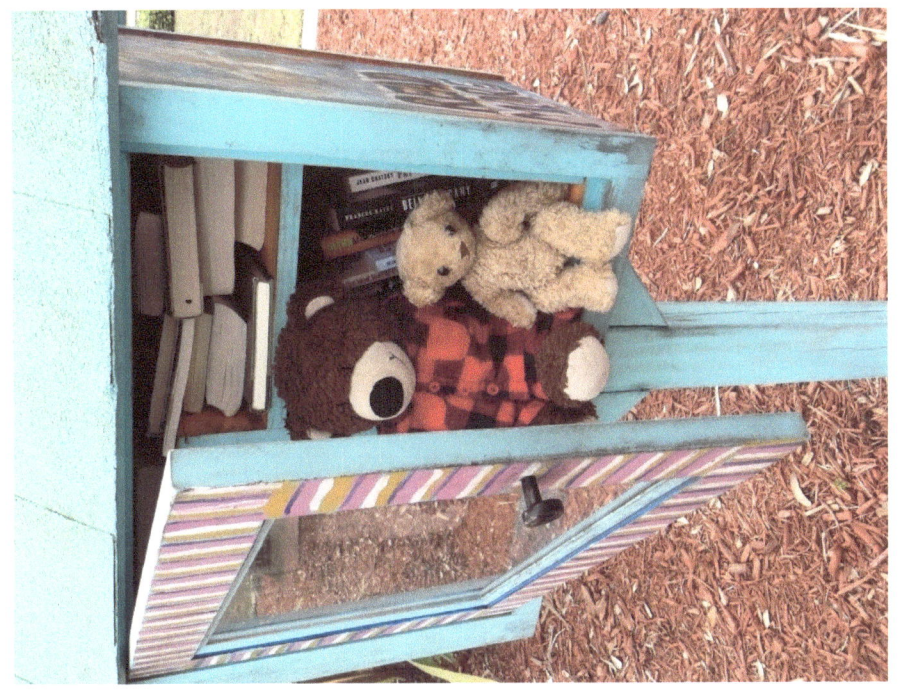

Here is Benedict and Takamatsu in the little free library in the park outside the library. Mom will put old drafts of her books in here when she is done with them in an effort to share her world with others, as broken and little as they are.

I am Benedict, actually. I am nine years old, and I am the main character, or MC of many of Mom's books. The other bear is Takamatsu, named after the vampire character of the same name in Midnight Madness. Takamatsu the vampire, or Taro, as he is more commonly called; collects stuffed toys, saving them from the trash because he believes that they embody the souls of lost ancestors. He keeps them in a shrine and honors them as often as possible.

The teddy bear Takamatsu is a teddy bear mom found in an indoor flea market that has since closed down. She fell in love with the bear because it had obviously been well loved by someone before it had been donated to sell. She saved the bear in the spirit of the character he was named after. He had become of her best friends since and is likely to star in his own books in the future. Mom has already begun taking photos of him and he goes with her to work sometimes, even when I can't. He is a smaller teddy bear and therefor can fit into smaller purses and bags.

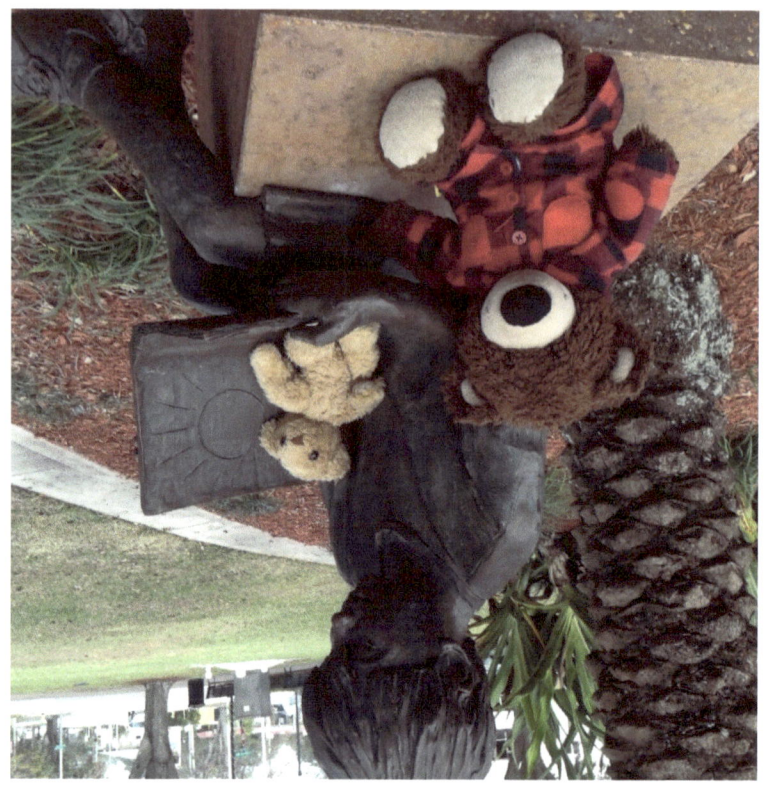

Here we are at a statue in the park outside the library. We love this statue because we love books. We love to read books and we love to write books. Books are our best friends and we are always on the hunt for new best friends, both in those written by others and ones waiting to be birthed from our own heads because they simply do not exist yet in the outside world.

Our books become an oasis; they usually seem to center around a small family of misfits in an otherwise hostile world. They are places where mom, and hopefully others, go to feel that somebody out there does care, even if the rest of the world seems to be cold and unfeeling. They are a place to wander and wonder, un-judged by others and hoping to find one's true place in the universe. They are filled with characters who do not know what they are doing but are trying the best they can to do as much good as possible regardless. It is a plea for people to just be good to other people. Hopefully people can see that in the strange plots and sometimes poorly written but passionately felt sentences. It is our hope to reach other people through our books, just as we find others through the books we read.

It is a desire for one writer to become one link in the great chainmail of literature, linked together with the great and the not so great in an effort to be heard. Hopefully, if we keep trying, it will actually grow into something big. Either way, we are happy for having been a part of the effort. Thank you for being a part of it with us by linking into our book.

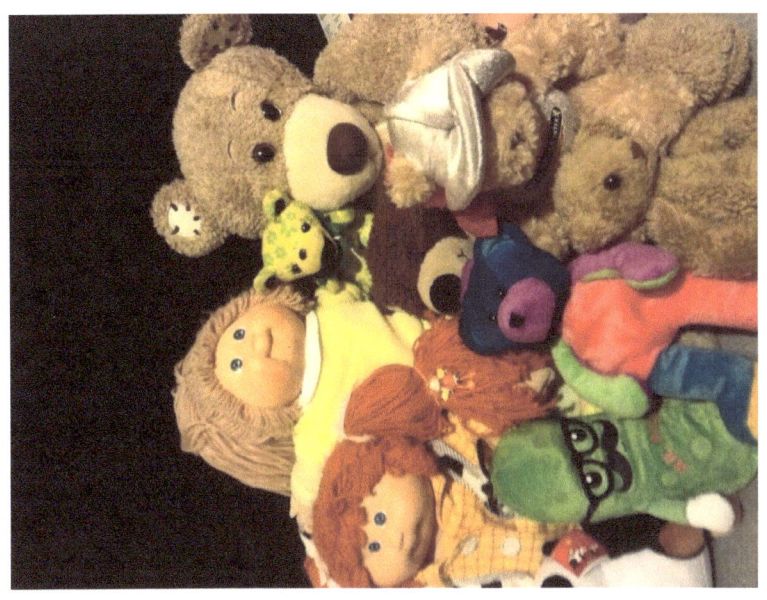

Here is a random group photo for your consideration. Some have moved on to other homes and have begun new stories. Some have remained in the house, for now or for good. Every plushie has a story and I believe it is up to us to work together to tell them. I challenge you to write such a story and be a part of this chainmail of worlds and photos. I wish you luck and hope you have fun on your journey.

We would love to see what you come up with.

We publish through amazon and create space, but even sharing through Facebook, or another social media would be fun. We love to look for books and characters that have been posted. If possible, contact my page and we can share creative writings together.

I am called Benedict the monastic Bear. Be warned. Mom is a generation Xer, we know something of social media and such, but we are nowhere near as adept with it as the younger generations are. We will do the best we can to answer any fried requests or the like as much as possible while keeping ourselves safe in the great frightening thing which in the internet.

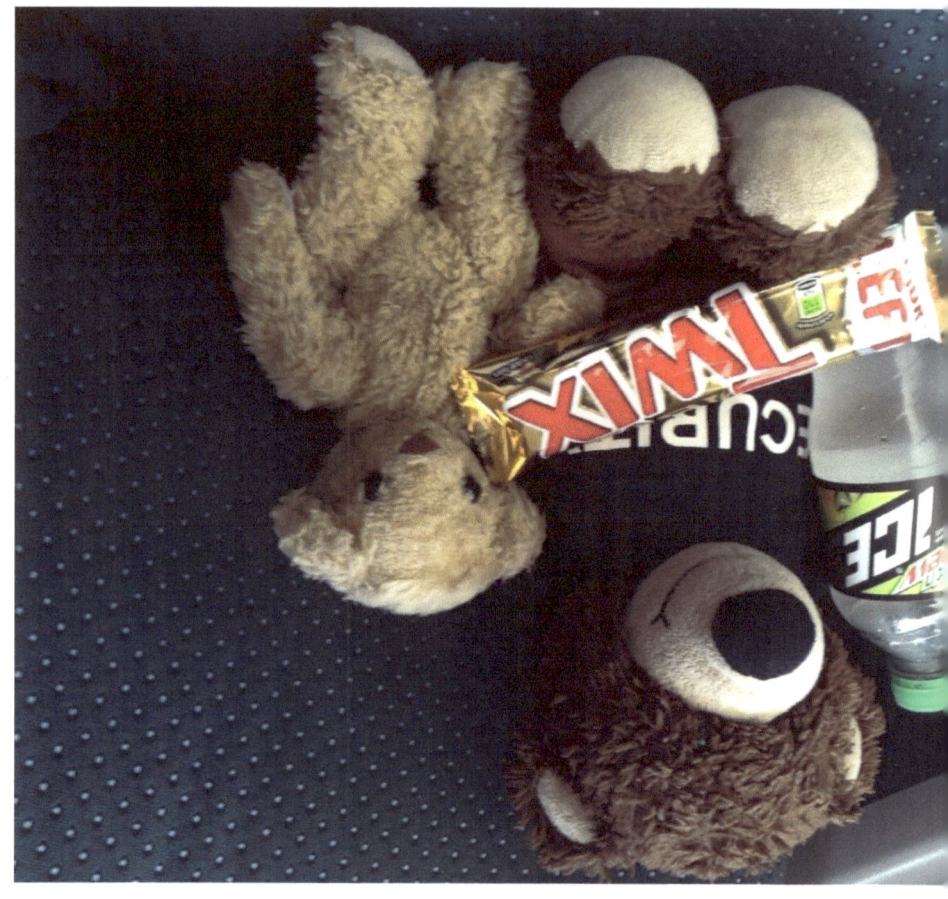

In the meantime, have some snacks with us. I promise we are working as hard as we can to be able to share these books with you. Here is a sneak peak from Teddy Bears at work, in which Mom attempt to share her first job with others in hopes that a usually invisible and underappreciated job gets noticed and appreciated. Did you know that whenever a patient gets put on a heart monitor, that there are people whose sole purpose is to watch all of the patients and keep them safe? That is what mom does and we illustrated this in a book with teddy bears for your education and information.

We must close for now. Mom sends her love and grateful thanks to you and so do I. Have a great day and I hope you make something fun.

www.ingramcontent.com/pod-product-compliance
Lightning Source LLC
Chambersburg PA
CBHW040351220526
45473CB00009B/2857